ABIDING
IN
GOD'S WORD

ABIDING
IN
GOD'S WORD

*How one women's spiritual journey gave her
the key to eternal life!*

MRS. BEVERLY CLAIBORNE

WESTBOW
PRESS®
A DIVISION OF THOMAS NELSON
& ZONDERVAN

WestBow Press books may be ordered through booksellers or by contacting:

WestBow Press
A Division of Thomas Nelson & Zondervan
1663 Liberty Drive
Bloomington, IN 47403
www.westbowpress.com
1 (866) 928-1240

Because of the dynamic nature of the Internet, any web addresses or links contained in this book may have changed since publication and may no longer be valid. The views expressed in this work are solely those of the author and do not necessarily reflect the views of the publisher, and the publisher hereby disclaims any responsibility for them.

Scripture quotations marked (NIV) are taken from the Holy Bible, New International Version®, NIV®. Copyright © 1973, 1978, 1984, 2011 by Biblica, Inc.™ Used by permission of Zondervan. All rights reserved worldwide. www.zondervan.com The "NIV" and "New International Version" are trademarks registered in the United States Patent and Trademark Office by Biblica, Inc.™

Scripture quotations marked (NLT) are taken from the Holy Bible, New Living Translation, copyright ©1996, 2004, 2015 by Tyndale House Foundation. Used by permission of Tyndale House Publishers, Inc., Carol Stream, Illinois 60188. All rights reserved.

Scripture quotations marked (NHEB) are taken from the New Heart English Bible.

Scripture quotations are from the ESV® Bible (The Holy Bible, English Standard Version®), copyright © 2001 by Crossway, a publishing ministry of Good News Publishers. Used by permission. All rights reserved.

Scripture quotations marked NKJV are taken from the New King James Version. Copyright © 1982 by Thomas Nelson, Inc. Used by permission. All rights reserved.

ISBN: 978-1-4497-3929-4 (sc)
ISBN: 978-1-4497-3930-0 (hc)
ISBN: 978-1-4497-3928-7 (e)

Library of Congress Control Number: 2012901985

Print information available on the last page.

WestBow Press rev. date: 06/01/2018

ACKNOWLEDGMENTS

*A*BIDING IN GOD'S WORD IS NOT JUST THE title of this book, but it is what God has called us to do.

I'd like to first thank God Almighty for his mercy and grace!

Special thanks to my spiritual mentor Dr. David Jeremiah and The Turning Point Ministries staff. The love and hospitality that I have received from this ministry have been both extraordinary and amazing. God will always send angels where they are needed. For those at the crossroads Dr. Jeremiah delivers the word of God to an ever changing world with passion.

To my spiritual mentors Dr. Charles F. Stanley, and Dr. Michael Youssef, PH.D. for always reminding me to not only listen to the Holy Spirit, but to believe in the Power of the Holy Spirit. Their biblical teachings have helped me gain a better understanding on what it means to abide.

Thanks to Pastors Creflo Dollar and Joyce Meyer for their boldness and stressing the importance of "Change".

Thanks to Dr. Arthur Belanger with the Open Bible Institute for always having a Christ like character and encouraging the students with joy.

Special thanks to my wonderful husband Cary who I love unconditionally and son Cameron for their love and support, for abiding in Christ along with me, and for understanding my purpose in writing this book.

Thanks to my dad Willie M. Stubbs for always providing and encouraging our family to love one another, your stern values, critical decisions, and military background will never be forgotten. Thanks all my siblings Webster, Barbara, Ronald, Donald, Christopher and Anita for always showing me how much you love me.

I can't thank Mia Redrick with Finding Definitions, LLC enough for her assistance and support during the writing of this book.

And last, but not least to my childhood friend Shereasher McDonald for always encouraging me to live with the assurance of God's faithfulness.

DEDICATION

*T*HIS BOOK IS DEDICATED TO MY BELOVED mother, Ruby Jean Stubbs. Thank you for not being afraid to demonstrate praise and worship and for stressing the importance of having a personal relationship with our Lord and Savior, Jesus Christ. Until we meet again, rest in peace.

CONTENTS

FOREWORD

*M*AKE SURE YOU'RE NOT MISSING THIS point for your life—read this book. Abiding in God's Word will be life changing and challenging for many Christians and non-Christians. It will give you tremendous insight as the writer shares even her own personal life experiences. This book is destined to be a classic on Christian living. I have witnessed the amazing transformation in Beverly as God has laid on her heart to share with the world the true meaning of abiding in Him! This is a must read as it will be life changing and give you a deeper understanding of the word *abide!*

Shereasher McDonald

President, Sports World Ministries, Inc.

I

WORLDLY LIVING

He that believes in the Son has everlasting life;
and he that believes not the Son shall not see
life; but the wrath of God abides on him.

—John 3:36 (NKJV)

*W*HAT COMES TO MIND WHEN YOU THINK
of the word "abide"? On a basic level, it means to live in a
place, although Merriam-Webster has a much more specific
meaning for the word. The dictionary lists the meaning
of "abide" as "to remain stable or fixed in a state" or "to
continue in a place."

So "abiding" means more than just complying. It means to be fixed
on a firm foundation in a special place that will hold us stable.
Abiding is about existing permanently in a place. That place may be

physical, like a home or a workplace. It may also be intangible, like a mindset or a deeply held belief. We all abide in one or more of these different places in our lives, and they all have a major impact on us. Just stop and think for a moment about the places you abide in. Most specifically, think about the mindset you spend most of your time in. Do you trust God at every turn?

The Bible also gives us an important meaning of "abide." It means endure, keep, and remain. John 15:10 (NKJV) explains this meaning to us: "If you keep My commandments, you shall abide in My love; even as I have kept my Father's commandments, and abide in His love."

In the spring of 2009, I began to notice more and more adversity in my life, which really frustrated me. After experiencing and witnessing several moral tribulations involving close friends and family members, much of my time was spent worrying about things I could not control—like other people's behavior and manners. I found myself mishandling almost every adversity that touched my life. I began praying, "God, take people out of my life who do not belong there and please keep the ones (and send others) you feel are needed." Surprisingly, many people I considered friends disappeared. I felt a separation between my friends and even certain family members. I now realize that that was God seeking me and answering my prayers.

When tragedy or difficult trials are imposed upon your life, you must be prepared to respond biblically, not as the world responds. After that desperate prayer, I started to read my Bible on a daily basis and to pray more. I began spending a lot of time watching Creflo Dollar (my former pastor) on television and listening to his *Battle of the Mind* CD over and over again. Both helped me to understand more about why I had lived as a carnal Christian for so long. (A carnal Christian is someone who believes in Jesus Christ and professes Him as their Savior but continues to live in a sinful, fleshly, and worldly way, doing things the Bible clearly says are wrong.)

Our Holy Bible goes into detail about how we must renew our minds in order to receive victory in this troubled world. Creflo Dollar's *Battle of the Mind* CD goes into details about renewing the mind and why it is critical to listen to the Word of God. I decided that it was time to take his advice about being "spirit-led." I kept hearing Dr. Dollar's voice saying, "Listen to the Holy Spirit so you will know what God wants for you."

When I attended his church in the early '90s, Creflo Dollar would end almost every sermon with Proverbs 4:7 (NKJV): Wisdom is the principal thing; Therefore get wisdom. And in all you'regetting, get understanding. I finally put that into practice. I followed the advice of an angel I speak about in later chapters, and now I'm a different person. Reading my Bible and developing a personal relationship with Jesus Christ changed my life dramatically. I prayed for forgiveness, forgave others, and spent hours each day with the Word.

That's when the Holy Spirit manifested in my life. It did not happen in my own strength. It was God's given grace. Experiencing the indwelling power of the Holy Spirit made me start walking in obedience.

2

ANGELS

For he will command his angels concerning you
to guard you in all your ways.

—Psalm 91:11 (NKJV)

NOT LONG AFTER I BEGAN TO LEARN MORE
about trusting God and following His Spirit,
I began to be more aware of His presence in my life. One
noticeable experience happened in a bookstore. It was very
subtle; if I had not been walking in obedience or listening to
the Holy Spirit, I might have missed it.

I had always wanted to see an angel. Even as a little girl, I
would look up at all the stars in the sky and think about angels.
Not long ago, a friend of mine showed me a photo of what
she thought was an angel. It was a huge silhouette on an old

dirt road in South Carolina. I thought, *Is this really an angel? Is it a nice angel?* My friend said that the photo hadn't been tampered with, and she hadn't noticed the silhouette when she snapped the photo of her grandmother's house (which looked like a house built in the late 1800s). That night I prayed to God, asking him to send the angel to me. Now do not misunderstand me when I speak about angels. I'm a scriptural believer and I do not worship them, however I do believe they are sent forth to minister to us. I could not tell you what an angel looks like because I've never seen one to my knowledge, however I have experienced their presence.

The next morning, I went to Barnes & Noble and found a book titled *Angels*. The cover with a sky-blue background and a large wing immediately drew my attention; I knew that this was the book I was supposed to purchase. Without paying attention to the author or the statement on the front cover (I later noted that he was a *New York Times* best-selling author), I began to read, looking up all the referenced Scriptures and reading at every opportunity; the Scriptures gave me so much truth and clarity about angels and their existence.

One Sunday afternoon perhaps two weeks after finishing the book, I was in my kitchen, preparing dinner and listening to the television. Just as I walked into the other room, a commercial came on and the name of the gentleman speaking caught my attention. It was Dr. David Jeremiah—the author of the angel book I'd been reading. I had never heard of Dr.

Jeremiah before, although he'd been preaching for decades. I finally read the acknowledgments in the book I'd purchased, and when I learned more details about the author, I knew God had answered my prayers about angels. In his book, Dr. David Jeremiah uses Scripture to unveil the remarkable truth about these agents of heaven and their role in our world and in our lives. Dr. Jeremiah's biblical teaching and leadership has changed my life.

While reading Dr. Jeremiah's book on Angels~several scriptures from the book of Hebrews really illuminated my spirit, namely 2:1-4 reads ˜ So we must listen very carefully to the truth we have heard, or we may drift away from it. For the message God delivered through angels has always stood firm, and every violation of the law and every act of disobedience was punished. So what makes us think we can escape if we ignore this great salvation that was first announced by the Lord Jesus himself and then delivered to us by those who heard him speak? And God confirmed the message by giving signs and wonders and various miracles and gifts of the Holy Spirit whenever he chose.(NLT)

God will always lead you to the truth and the things He wants you to see and learn. The key is that you must also set your mind on things above. 1 Peter 1:13-16(NKJV) tells us to

> gird up the loins of your mind, be sober, and
> rest *your* hope fully upon the grace that is to be
> brought to you at the revelation of Jesus Christ;

as obedient children, not conforming yourselves
to the former lusts, *as* in your ignorance; but as
He who called you *is* holy, you also be holy in
all your conduct, because it is written, **"Be holy,
for I am holy."**

I stopped going to church regularly and only read my bible in
church on Sundays. "Yep!" I was a Sunday Christian. I was
living life the way I wanted to live it, without total adoration
for God.

I judged others but failed to examine my own spiritual condition,
ignoring the Holy Spirit that dwells in me. One may ask what
is living carnally? Believers who live centered around their own
needs and desires with a self-obsessed mind not a mind that is
open to God. Romans 8:6-8 (NKJV) tells us For to be carnally
minded is death; but to be spiritually minded is life and peace.
Because the carnal mind is enmity against God: for it is not
subject to the law of God, neither indeed can be. So then they
that are in the flesh cannot please God.

However, once I set my mind to obey the words of God and to
walk humbly with Him, my life changed for the better. Now I
realize it was God seeking me the entire time. He could not speak
to me spiritually until now, because I was not ready to receive
it according to 1 Corinthians 3. Trusting in God for everything
may be one of the most difficult decisions a believer makes.
However, once you make up your mind that you are going to

abide continuously in God's Word, giving every moment and thought to Him is not difficult. We must know and understand that we cannot do this within our own natural beings. It's the Holy Spirit who guides us and shapes our paths.

In 1 Thessalonians 5:17 (NKJV), Paul tells us to "pray without ceasing." While this doesn't mean that we need to spend literally every moment on our knees in prayer, it does mean that God's presence should light up every thought we have and everything we do.

You may have seen those colorful bracelets that first became popular among young Christians in the 1990s. They come in various colors and have the letters *WWJD* on them. The letters stand for the phrase "What would Jesus do?" Try to imagine how your actions would change if you thought about what Jesus would do every time you did something. Luke 12:12 (NKJV) tells us, "For the Holy Spirit will teach you in that very hour what you ought to say."

3

PEACE

Be anxious for nothing, but in everything by prayer and supplication, with thanksgiving, let your requests be made known to God; and the peace of God, which surpasses all understanding, will guard your hearts and minds through Christ Jesus.

—Philippians 4:6-7 (NKJV)

*R*EMEMBER THE LAST TIME YOU FELT ANTSY and didn't know why? As human beings, we need rest. Sometimes we have things on our minds that simply prevent us from getting any rest at all. Other times, we rest so much that we find it hard to get out of bed to do the things we should be doing. Both are serious problems, and both can be caused by anxiety.

I remember one Sunday morning when I was in my teens and my mother was getting ready for church. She and I wore the same shoe size and often wore one another's shoes. She came into my bedroom, turned on the light, and started rooting around in my closet, looking for a pair of shoes to borrow. I had been out late partying the night before, and when she turned that light on, I rolled over and pulled the covers over my head.

"Turn the light off," I mumbled.

"I'm not turning out the light," my mother answered calmly. "I'm going to take my time and find a pair of shoes that I like, and I'm going to church. You need to get up and go with me."

In that moment, all I could think about was trying to rest, because I had expended all of my energies living a worldly life. I wanted to rest from everything I had done the night before. I didn't want to get up and go to church, but my mother was right. I couldn't rest when God was waiting on me. Instead of lying in bed, I should have been seeking His presence.

None of us can truly rest until we abide in Christ. Any rest we take will be sporadic at best, and we'll always wonder what will happen next. Carnal Christians lack peace because they haven't allowed Christ to truly take up residence in their lives full time. God wants us to be peaceful. He wants us to experience peace in our lives and peace about death and going to heaven.

While Christ was still on earth, He said, "Peace I leave with you, my peace I give to you; not as the world gives do I give to you. Let not your heart be troubled, neither let it be afraid."(John 14:27) NKJV

Peace is one of God's gifts—something we can all have if we put our pride aside and allow the Holy Spirit to have complete control over our lives. This is why saved Christians can overcome adversities easier than carnal Christians—they demonstrate peace even when it seems like their world is caving in on them. They are like Shadrach, Meshach, and Abednego in the fiery furnace. Instead of worrying about their predicament, they prayed and praised God.

Just think about what life would be like if you didn't worry so much. What if you listened to God and his ministering angels? Would your life be different? I remember thinking shortly before my mother died that she seemed very much at peace. Once while visiting mother in the hospital, she asked me to take out a tablet and write down how she wanted to be buried.

When she asked me to do it, I said, "Oh, Mom, everything is going to be all right."

She was persistent, however. Knowing that I needed to be strong for her, I grabbed a pen and wrote down the details about how she wanted to be buried. Most importantly, she said, "Beverly, make sure you put a Bible in my hand." It was extremely hard to write the details, I was reluctant to do it—it felt as if I was engraving her tomb stone, I never experienced hurt like this before. During that time I felt like her death was final, but after listening to Dr. David Jeremiah's sermon from the book of Luke, I experienced a since of freedom and closure like never before. Now, I'm encouraged and look forward to seeing her again.

To this day, I can still see her holding that white Bible. It meant so much to her—now I know why. When my mother died, I didn't know God, but she did. I wondered how she got the strength not to cry while telling me these things or going through her cancer treatments.

For over twenty years I would frequently cry over her death. It wasn't until after I read Dr. Jeremiah's book on angels and listened to his CDs titled *Revealing the Mysteries of Heaven*—the CD *Where Are They Now?* stands out in my mind—that many of my questions were answered. Dr. Jeremiah speaks of two men contrasted in life from Luke 16:19-31. (NKJV) Preaching straight from the scriptures about "The Rich man and Lazarus". Dr. Jeremiah stresses~ this is not the Lazarus that was raised from the dead, but another Lazarus.

The Scriptures reveal a rich man who was clothed in purple and fine linen and fared sumptuously every day. There was a certain beggar named Lazarus, full of sores, who laid at his gate, desiring to be fed with the crumbs which fell from the rich man's table. The beggar died, and was carried by the angels to Abraham's bosom. The rich man also died and was buried. And being in torments in Hades, he lifted up his eyes and saw Abraham afar off, and Lazarus in his bosom. "Then the rich man cried and said, 'Father Abraham, have mercy on me, and send Lazarus that he may dip the tip of his finger in water and cool my tongue; for I am tormented in this flame.' But Abraham said, 'Son, remember that in your lifetime you received your good things, and likewise Lazarus evil things; but now he is comforted and you are tormented. And besides all this, between us and you there is a great gulf fixed, so that those who want to pass from here to you cannot, nor can those from there pass to us. When unbelievers die they go to Hades, a place of torment, when believers die the angels take them to heaven, a placed called paradise. "Then he said, 'I beg you therefore, father, that you would send him to my father's house, for I have five brothers, that he may testify to them, lest they also come to this place of torment.' Abraham said to him, 'They have Moses and the prophets; let them hear them.' And the rich man said, 'No, father Abraham; but if one goes to them from the dead, they will repent.' But he said to him, 'If they do not hear Moses and the prophets, neither will they be persuaded though one rise from the dead." Revelations 20:13-14 (NKJV) tells more. Seeing the change of life style in my mom and knowing she was a believer is comforting.

Now I feel in my heart such incredible strength, confidence, and gladness that she is with the Lord. God gives us His grace in the hour we need it.

I was so burdened by her death because I was not seeking God at that time. I did not have a personal relationship yet. God wants us to seek Him first, and lean not on our own understanding. In Matthew 6:33 (NKJV), He commands, "Seek first the kingdom of God And His righteousness."

Peace is commonly defined as the sense of calm, tranquility, quietness, bliss, contentment, and well-being that we feel when things are going well. Godly peace cannot be produced on a human level. God's grace is a privileged gift given as a divine right.

I remember having a conversation with Mom in the kitchen one day. She walked up to me and asked, "Don't you want to go?"

"Go where?" I asked.

She said, "To heaven."

I said yes at the time, but truthfully I only said it because I thought that was what she wanted to hear. I was still living carnally.

Carnal Christians will always have that irritating little suspicion that there's something missing. They will always question themselves and blame others for their own unhappiness, constantly ignoring the Holy Spirit. God's peace is always available, and there is no limit to it. There are conditions for receiving peace: trusting God, turning from sin, enduring the refining process, doing good deeds, and living by the Word. God will infuse us with His peace and grace. And that has a wonderful way of eliminating anxiety.

4

SPIRITUAL AWARENESS

The lamp of the body is the eye. If therefore, your eye is good, your whole body shall be full of light. But if your eye is bad, your whole body will be full of darkness. If therefore the light in you is darkness, how great is that darkness!

—Matthew 6:22-24 (NKJV)

*W*HAT KINDS OF THINGS DO YOU SPEND most of your time thinking about?

Be honest as you ponder this question, although spiritual blindness caused by worldly living can make honesty difficult. Most people who are living in the world expend the majority of their energy thinking about their bank accounts, stock portfolios, entertainment, cars, houses, relatives, and friends. Or they spend their time trying to figure out how a misunderstood conversation turned into a full-blown argument. Focusing on all of these material things is an indication of worldly living.

Although proclaiming to be a Christian, in reality I was not living like one. For years I grieved the Holy Spirit allowing corrupt words to proceed out of my mouth, failing to put away bitterness and anger. Why? As Christians we have the tendency to take Satan's superiority lightly. As Paul says in Ephesians 2:2 (NKJV), still dead in trespasses and sin walking according to the course of this world, according to the prince of the power of the air (Satan), the spirit who now works in the sons of disobedience. Satan structures the world's system of thinking and has demons following him. He has people on his team, but they are not being attacked.

Why?

They are already on his side.

Satan's strategy is to distract you from God's will for your life. I fell into a continual pattern of sin and focused most of my time on worldly things. I started to hang out with people who looked beautiful on the outside, but their hearts where full of deceit. We spent so much time talking about ourselves, handbags, the latest fashions, gossip—you name it. We talked about everything except my Lord and Savior, Jesus Christ. We totally failed to acknowledge our real purpose in life, and that is to serve God!

I began to hurt, knowing I was not honoring God. I knew something was not right. My sister Anita kept asking me what was wrong. She said, "Why are you complaining so much? If I had your life, I would be so happy."

The truth was that Anita only saw the external me, not the internal me. I started to hate what I viewed and discussed as having fun. Something inside me just didn't feel peaceful. That something was the Holy Spirit. God has His way of getting our attention—by revealing our sins in our life. Most people just hum away and ignore Him, which I had done several times in the past. This time was different, however. I began to drift away from certain people, and the more I sought advice in ungodly places, the more depressed I became. Be careful who you seek advice from; ungodly women give ungodly advice.

The bible tells us in Proverbs 12:5-6 (NKJV), "The thoughts of the righteous are just, but guidance from the wicked leads to deceit. The words of the wicked are a deadly ambush, but the speech of the upright rescues them."

We all have to be careful who we take advice from. It's only natural that we reach out to others during times of trouble, but reaching out to the wrong people can ruin our lives. God puts certain people in our lives to guide us, but He isn't the only one who allows the words and works of others to affect us. Satan also places people in our lives, although the people he places there are meant to mislead us. We even have to be discerning with the churches we attend and the pastors who lead us, always remembering that they are human as well.

In Exodus 20:17 (NKJV), God warns us not to covet. What is that? *Unlawful desires and thoughts and loving things more than people* describes it best.

Yes, covet is one of the Ten Commandments most people seem to forget. Now the purpose of this commandment is for us to love with a pure heart, from a good conscience, and with sincere faith. Have you ever pretended to like someone and deep down you could not stand to be in their presence? I mean you wished they would just disappear or that you could give him or her a beat down and pray about it later. Well there are two things happening. 1) You're letting Satan steal your joy and 2) God is revealing the true condition of your heart. Satan knows you and what you will and will not react to. The bottom line is this. We must acknowledge that we are children of wrath, and this sin nature produces all kinds of sinful acts. Failure to acknowledge this truth will cause you to continue to struggle with the same problems. You must repent. God knows our hearts; we can fool just about anyone but Him. As believers, we have this confidence: God is always in complete control. When God allows Satan to light the furnace, he's always there to control the thermostat!

God positions people in our lives that are filled with His spirit, but we have to open our hearts and listen to them;

stop turning them away when God sends them to help you. Often we are so busy doing things our way; we miss out on God's messengers. How do you know it's from God? Pray about it! It will be revealed again and again His way, not in an ungodly way. Satan knows this so he will position people to stop the blessings from flowing—he may even use people who are closest to us to hinder what God wants. Remember in Matthew 16 when Jesus predicts his death and resurrection? Peter tried to stop him

> From that time Jesus began to show to His disciples that He must go to Jerusalem, and suffer many things from the elders and chief priests and scribes, and be killed, and be raised the third day.
>
> Peter took Him aside and began to rebuke Him, saying, "Far be it from You, Lord; this shall not happen to You!"
>
> But He turned and said to Peter, "Get behind Me, Satan! You are an offense to Me, for you are not mindful of the things of God, but the things of men."

Hebrews 13:4-5 (NKJV) and Luke 12 talk more about covetousness. And Proverbs 28:20 (NKJV) says, "Faithful man will abound with blessings, but he who hastens to be rich will not go unpunished."

The Bible continually warns us not to be greedy, although Luke 16:14-15 (NKJV) tells us that the Pharisees certainly were.

> Now the Pharisees, who were lovers of money, also heard all these things, and they derided Him. And Jesus said to them, "You are those who justify yourselves before men, but God knows your hearts. For what is highly esteemed among men is an abomination in the sight of God."

The Pharisees were so earthbound that all they could see were their worldly possessions. God warns us against this lifestyle. 1 Corinthians 10:31 (NKJV) reads, "Whatever you do, whether you eat or drink, or whatever you do, do it all to the glory of God."

The problem begins for us when we do things for our own glory and indulge our worldly lifestyle. Of course trials like the ones caused by Satan and those he chooses to use in evil ways (like the Pharisees) are a part of life. God allows these trials so that we may become stronger. He allows us to experience spiritual blindness for a time, but our growth requires us to take the next step. Normally when you experience a trial it's

God trying to get you to release something that you want to holding onto; He wants you to let it go.

There are more and more Christians unknowingly living in blindness. In the Bible, Jesus's brother James shares with us in the very first chapter of James, verses 13-15.

> No one undergoing a trial should say, "I am being tempted by God." For God is not tempted by evil, and He Himself doesn't tempt anyone. But each person is tempted when he is drawn away and enticed by his own evil desires. Then after desire has conceived, it gives birth to sin, and when sin is fully grown, it gives birth to death.

All Satan needs is a seed to grow inside you, and that seed will come directly from worldly life. We all have a choice to make: whether we want to lay our treasure on heaven or on earth. We can choose whether we are going to live in the light or in the darkness and whether we will serve God or money, but we can't choose both of these options.

Only true repentance will save you—not by remorse or reformation but a voluntary and sincere change of heart. Jesus said in John 15:16 (NKJV).

> You have not chosen me—for I have chosen you, and ordained you, that you should go and bring forth fruit, and that your fruit should remain: that what so ever you ask in my name, he may give it to you.

Now let's reflect for a minute. Has God given you grace? Are you walking in obedience according to words of the Holy Bible? Are you living like a true Christian or a carnal Christian? God knows the truth about us, so if you lie, you are only fooling yourself. Once we were slaves and strangers to the covenant, but Jesus paid the price for our freedom a long time ago.

We are all victims of the impressions that our culture makes upon us. Worldly ambition has a strong fascination for us, and the spell of materialism is very hard to break. Making the right choice is very difficult, but it can be done as long as we let the Spirit of God lead us and dwell in us. Choose where to lay your treasure, "for where your treasure is, that's where your heart will be also."

5

FAITH

And suddenly a great tempest arose on the sea, so that the boat was covered with the waves. But Jesus was asleep. Then His disciples came to Him and awoke Him, saying, "Lord, save us! We are perishing!" But He said to them, "Why are you fearful, O you of little faith?"

—Matthew 8:24-26 (NKJV)

*G*OD HAS THE ABILITY TO SHAKE UP ANYthing He wants to at any given time. We know God used earthquakes as signs several times in the Bible, so why wouldn't He use them as signs for His believers today?

One problem our world faces is that too many Christians don't have the faith that they should. We all spend time looking for a less incredible explanation to something amazing that happens to us. After all, why would God communicate directly with us?

But the point is not why God would communicate directly with each one of us; it is that so many of us don't think He does. Instead we come up with other ways to explain God's signs. God tells us in Ephesians 2:8-9 (NKJV), "For by grace you have been saved through faith, and that not of yourselves; it is the gift of God, not of works, lest anyone should boast."

There's also another key word in that verse. The word *grace* explains that God didn't have to save any of us. He decided that he wanted to, so He extended us grace, which is the gift of eternal life, a gift none of us ever deserved.

As we learn to accept God's grace, it is also important to get our priorities straight. I urge everyone to listen to Dr. Jeremiah's CD *Captured by Grace*. Grace is an abstract idea until it happens to you. Dr. Jeremiah is the senior pastor of Shadow Mountain Community Church in San Diego, California. His teachings have really touched me recently, and he emphasizes the need for getting our priorities straight.

Dr. Jeremiah suggests a good activity to help us all get our priorities straight. Ask this question: If you were given one hour to evacuate your home and were allowed one suitcase to hold your belongings, what would you take?

The point is to force people to think about priorities. Answers usually include things like family photo albums, keepsake jewelry, valued gifts, and important documents. Today one would probably include one's laptop and cell phone!

Everything in life is not equally important, nor is everything in the kingdom of God on the same plane. Of three important virtues—faith, hope, and love—Paul said that love was the greatest. Jesus revealed the first and second most important commandments out of the hundreds of commandments in Israel's canon. You shall love the Lord your God with all your heart, with all your soul, and with all your mind. This is the first and great commandment. And the second is like it: You shall love your neighbor as yourself. Matthew 22:37-39 (NKJV).

Today's economic recession has caused many people to think afresh about what is most important in their life. When funds are limited, or the future looks scary, we begin to make choices: God, spouse, family, neighbors, health, savings . . . Be aware of changes and choices you are making in these challenging days. Then be true to yourself and hold on to those priorities!

Signs from God aren't as rare as you think, but Christians who have enough faith to believe in those signs are, unfortunately, becoming rarer by the day. What do you think when someone tells you he or she has received a sign from God? Unfortunately the world has desensitized us to many of these signs. Hollywood has shown us almost everything there is to see, and science has a way of explaining away everything. We have all seen so much that the thought of God communicating with us just seems too incredible. Sometimes, however, God's communications aren't as grand as an earthquake. Sometimes they can be found in a still, small voice. I remember one day I was watching Day Star, one of the Christian networks, when I heard a gentleman talking about his encounter with an angel. Hebrews 1:1-3 (NKJV) comes to mind. I asked myself out loud, "What angel has been with me?"

In that precise moment, I heard a soft voice say the name "Gabriel". I immediately turned the television off and went to sit down in my dining room where I had my Bible opened, and I reached for it. I heard the voice very clearly say, "Why do you reach for your Bible? Don't you believe?"

My hand froze on the Bible; then I let it go and sat still, waiting. I could tell I was not alone; a spirit was present. I asked the angel why he was there, and he began to speak, telling me what I was supposed to do. He said, "I've been sent by the Father to make sure you follow through with your assignment." I asked what my assignment was, and then the angel told me, "Restore peace among families, encourage women to be strong, children to become leaders, and men to become warriors and leaders, and to tell them about Him."

Speaking of fear and trembling, I could feel the hairs stand all over my body. I was home alone that afternoon, and I will never forget it; I experienced the amazing, peaceful presence of an angel. This caused a dramatic change in my life. I had received a message from God, and whether or not it was an angel or the Holy Spirit speaking to me, I had to be in that place at that moment in time for the message to come across. That event is what motivated me to write this book. I had never even thought about writing a book before this experience.

God always finds a way to slip His message in right where it needs to be. He will come to you in the hour when you are most able to hear Him, but you must have the faith to believe that He will.

Carnal Christians (1 Corinthians 3) are too busy telling Him what they want. They cannot hear His advice because Satan has them too busy and consumed with worldly stuff. They cannot hear His plan for their life. He has a plan that is far better than any plan you have, but you have to believe that He has that plan and is communicating it to you.

The Gospels are full of stories about people whose faith got them what they wanted. Peter was able to walk on water until the moment his faith faltered. Then he sank and had to be pulled up by Jesus. In Luke 8:43-48 (NKJV), we have the story of a woman who had a bleeding disorder for twelve years. She believed that if she could just touch Jesus's cloak, she would be healed—and she was. Jesus even told her, "Be of good cheer, daughter; your faith has made you well."

Faith is an amazing source of power that too many Christians aren't using. It's the one muscle in our body that has the potential to be the strongest, but it's weak and flabby. It atrophied from lack of use.

Has God left you any messages recently? He knows what kinds of things you will respond to, and He knows how to get through to you. However, if you harden your heart and stop believing that He will speak to you, then you'll miss out on His great plans for you.

I strongly recommend that all Christians read and meditate on Luke 1 and 2. We all know those chapters. They contain the birth of Christ, but this truth is important for those who think Jesus was just a prophet. Within these chapters you will find the following stories: Mary's visit to Elizabeth, the birth of John the Baptist, Zechariah's prophecy, Jesus's birth, the shepherds and the angels, Jesus being presented in the temple, the prophecies of Simeon and Anna, and Jesus speaking with the teachers.

Faith is something we're all born with, but unfortunately somewhere along the way we forget to use it. As small children, we believe Mom or Dad will always keep us from falling, but then one day our parents let us down. Our human parents are just that: human. They, along with other people in our lives, are bound to let us down sometimes. But God never will let us down. Even if He says no—and oftentimes He will—we have to trust and believe that He makes the best decision for our lives, even if we don't understand the reason. We must activate our faith when we say to Jesus, "I choose to see You as bigger than my negative situation, the answer to my need, and the solution to all my problems."

If you ask God to turn any unbelief in your heart into belief—and He knows that you truly believe—that alone will activate your faith. Just believe that God will work wonders in your life, and He certainly will.

6

SPIRITUAL AMNESIA

These people draw near to Me with their mouth
and honor Me with their lips, but their heart
is far from Me. And in vain they worship Me,
teaching as doctrines and the commandments
of men.

—Isaiah 29:13 (NHEB)

*W*HEN WAS THE LAST TIME YOU CLEANED
house? I mean, *really* cleaned house. When was the last time
you cleaned out the basement, the attic, or the garage? Take
a few moments and think about the things you have stored
there. Most people stash things they don't intend on using for
a long time, things like old baby clothes or furniture. What
about that old piece of exercise equipment? No matter what
things you have put out of sight, they are still in your house.

You might have no intention of ever using them again, but they are still lurking there, in the dark.

What happens if a flood pours water into your home? Afterward, if you don't take the time to air out all of those things you have in storage, then you could have a real mold problem on your hands. Mold is unhealthy and it can make you sick, even if you don't know it's there. But how much easier would that flood have been if you didn't have all that junk stashed away in the corners of your home?

Many Christians have this same problem. They continue to walk around with all of the old sin patterns in their heads. In order to grow in God's Word, we have to spend time in it.

Carnal Christians live in a state of spiritual amnesia, ignoring their sins constantly. Dr. Michael Youssef describes an opinion of shadow spirituality in his book ~ *The Spirituality That Heals.*

On page 3, Dr. Youssef states:

> The New Age movement, perhaps more than any other entity, does the most to combine the human desire for healing with a form of spirituality. Building on the endorsement of many of Hollywood's best known celebrities,

the New Age movement has made spirituality something that is not only acceptable, but highly desirable.

But this is spirituality only in the loosest sense. In truth it is "shadow spirituality"—merely a shadow of the real thing. Don't allow these false teachers to mislead you. We need to lay hold of the only true spirituality there is—the only form of spiritual power that genuinely heals. We need the discernment to recognize the differences between shadow spirituality and the true spirituality of God. He says it is only in God's true spirituality that we find solace for our heart's deepest longings—healing for our soul, peace for our mind and comfort for our emotions. That healing, peace and comfort come only when we are committed to the pursuit of true spirituality.

Shadow spirituality is defined as the type of spirituality in which a person believes an individual can do all sorts of evil but still be a good person in his or her heart of hearts.

Remember that evil deeds flow from an evil heart.

Jesus said, "By the fruit you will recognize them" (Matthew 7:20 NKJV).

The Bible tells us in Matthew 7:18-21 (NKJV):

> "A good tree cannot bear bad fruit, nor can a bad tree bear good fruit. Every tree that does not bear good fruit is cut down and thrown into the fire. Therefore by their fruits you will know them. Not everyone who says to Me, 'Lord, Lord,' shall enter the kingdom of heaven, but he who does the will of My Father in Heaven."

Dr. Youssef is the founding rector of The Church Of The Apostles, in Atlanta, and president of an international broadcast ministry named Leading The Way. He stresses the importance of faith and the healing power that comes from the Holy Spirit in his book *Heal Me O God*. Brand this truth into your heart today from this book:

> The Holy Spirit possesses a dynamite-like power that works within a believer to blast out anything that is unlike God. It is not a power that exalts one person above. It does not manipulate or control others. Instead, the Holy Spirit uses His power to break us. The more we get self out of the way and yield our will to His, the more powerfully He is able to pour Himself through us to others, and the more powerfully He is able to transform our lives. We are merely the

conduits, the channels that God's power moves through.

When Christians first meet Christ or decide to dedicate themselves to church, they repent and suddenly feel changed. This change is short-lived in a number Christians, however. These Christians usually fall back into their old ways of living. They start enjoying God's blessings and forget about their past and how God changed them, which leads to spiritual blindness. Most have never experienced the true transformation—and fail to yield to the indwelling power of the Holy Spirit. Due to a continual pattern of rebellion and being reluctant to renewing their mind with the Word, they do not and cannot receive the full blessing from God; their flesh is unwilling.

Dr. Youssef exposes "shadow spirituality" in his book *Heal Me, O'God. This book is life changing and will guide you to authentic healing through the manifestation of the fruit of the Spirit in a fresh new way. You will embark on a journey toward personal healing and restoration of relationships.*

Look around and you'll be amazed at all the manifestations of the "self" movement, including self-actualization, self-empowerment, and self-improvement. It is as if all the answers to your problems are to be found by looking within. But this is spirituality only in the loosest sense. In truth, it is "shadow spirituality"—merely a shadow of the real thing. Shadow spirituality asks individuals to look inward, to put themselves at the center of the universe while pushing God so far to the fringes that He is left out of the picture. What remains is a spirituality of self. In other words shadow spirituality replaces the God of the universe with the "god within." This god is NOT the triune God revealed in the Bible, but rather a force that supposedly compels a person to improve himself. This god is nothing more than the human ability to learn, grow, and develop—all which are God's gifts to people. None of these abilities, however, is capable of regenerating the human heart. Only God has that power.

Movie stars, celebrities, and individuals who put themselves on pedestals are often people with high self-esteem—or should I say, they esteem themselves highly. They want to be served but have a problem serving others. Now don't misunderstand what I'm saying. I'm not knocking celebrities. I'm just making a point about individuals who think of themselves more highly than they ought to. Not all celebrities are like this; only the spiritually amnesiac. People change after they get what they want from God, often refusing to be humble and forgetting the Creator who helped them along the way.

The apostle Paul says in Romans 12:1-2 (NKJV):

> I beseech you, therefore, brethren, by the mercies of God, that you present your bodies a living sacrifice, holy, acceptable to God, which is your reasonable service. And do not be conformed to this world, but be transformed by the renewing

of your mind, that you may prove what is that good and acceptable and perfect will of God.

In Romans 12:3 (NKJV), Paul continues:

For I say, through the grace given unto me, to every man that is among you, not to think of himself more highly than he ought to think; but to think soberly, according as God hath dealt to every man the measure of faith.

Some Christians become humble for a while; they truly feel the blessing. As time goes on, however, they get spiritual amnesia, especially when the blessings are continuous. If Satan can entangle us in mixed-up priorities and false expectations regarding people and time, then he will have you in a trap. If Satan can wrap you up with a preoccupation about your own needs, your own schedule, and your own ambitions, he will have succeeded in drawing you away from reliance upon the Holy Spirit.

We should always give God the glory. Humility is a must when surrendering to God. The key word in Proverbs is *wisdom*, defined in Webster's dictionary as "having or showing discernment and good judgment." However a godly life in an ungodly world is no simple assignment. Many of our young people today are not living by biblical principles and often respond and make worldly decisions based on the world's view. They are not thinking about heaven as their future, and as a result often make bad decisions due to not placing God first in their lives. Why? Frequently this is due to the way they were raised. Often people judge others on how successful they are financially and not by their hearts or the fruit that they bear, failing to examine spiritually.

Proverbs 18:12-13 (NKJV) tells us, "Haughtiness goes before destruction; humility precedes honor. Spouting off before listening to the facts is both shameful and foolish."

God's change in your life is meant to allow you to live spiritually, not judgmentally. Being blessed is not cause to start looking down our noses at others but rather to love our fellow human beings and treat them as Jesus would have.

1 John 2:4 (NKJV)

> Now by this we know that we know Him, if we keep His commandments. He who says, "I know Him," and does not keep His commandments, is a liar, and the truth is not in him. But whoever keeps His word, truly the love of God is perfected in him. By this we know that we are abiding in Him. He who says he abides in Him ought himself also to walk just as He walked.

No one on earth is perfect; however through the gift of the Holy Spirit, which only comes through Jesus Christ, we can begin to see how godliness can be accomplished. Without God's grace, you will continue walking in the world. I'm a living witness of this truth.

The only way we can break free from our spiritual amnesia is to take the time to identify our spiritual condition. When God gives you grace, you immediately start to see and feel the difference between the world's way of living and the godly way He demands us to live. It all starts with forgiveness and mercy, not a passing forgiveness just to please others but genuine forgiveness that pleases God.

Spiritual amnesia prevents us from seeing how prevalent sin is in our lives. When you continually hurt loved ones and refuse to acknowledge their pain, when you intentionally make people feel bad or have an all-about-me attitude, you have fallen into spiritual amnesia.

This behavior of selfishness is not pleasing to God. It truly offends Him.

The Bible says in James 3:14-17 (NKJV)

> If you have bitter envy and self-seeking in your hearts, do not boast and lie against the truth. This behavior does not descend from above, but is earthly sensual, and demonic. For where envy and self-seeking exist, confusion and every

evil thing are there. But the wisdom that is from above is first pure, then peaceable, gentle, willing to yield, full of mercy and good fruits, without partiality and without hypocrisy.

God feels that if you've done it to the least of them, you've done it to Him. Christians still living in darkness do not see this as a problem. They are so full of pride that they don't even try to feel anyone else's pain. Often Satan keeps them so busy they don't even acknowledge the feelings of others. Some may realize they are sinning and still do not care. As long as they get what they want, they don't care whose heart they break. In reality, they are just killing their own souls. They get offended when you bring ungodly behavior to their attention.

Pride will keep you out of heaven and, even worse, send you to hell. So the next time you say, "My pride just won't allow me to do it," when it comes to forgiving someone, just know that it's all part of Satan's evil plan to keep you in bondage. Now might be a good time to look in the mirror and reflect on how you treat others.

Ask yourself this: Am I on my way to heaven or hell? Do I abide in the Word or am I being led by evil?

The more time we spend studying God's Word, the more we will begin to realize that sin hurts.

God tell us in 1 John 2:9-11 (NKJV):

> He who says he is in the light, and hates his brother, is in darkness until now. He who loves his brother abides in the light, and there is no cause for stumbling in him. But he who hates his brother is in darkness and walks in darkness, and does not know where he is going, because the darkness has blinded his eyes.

Only when the veil of spiritual blindness is lifted can we begin to see the way we are supposed to live. We need to let God's Word light our paths so that we can see in the darkness of this world.

7

OVERCOMING SATAN

Then the Lord God called to Adam and said to him, "Where are you?" So he said, "I heard Your voice in the garden, and I was afraid because I was naked; and I hid myself." And He said, "Who told you that you were naked? Have you eaten from the tree of which I commanded you that you should not eat?" Then the man said, "The woman whom you gave to be with me, she gave me of the tree, and I ate." And the Lord God said to the woman, "What is this you have done?" The woman said, "The serpent deceived me, and I ate."

—Genesis 3:9-12 (NKJV)

*W*HAT'S THE FIRST THING WE DO WHEN someone asks us if we've done something wrong?

It's only natural that we look for someone else to blame; it's common and has been going on since the beginning of time (although things were much simpler back then). Eve was the only one in the garden of Eden with Adam so he blamed her and she blamed Satan.

It's certainly easy to pass the buck, but no one gets off that easily in God's book. True, Satan does deceive us, but we all play a role in our own deception. Our worldly lives open us up to all of this deception, and Satan will take advantage of it. After all, what's the second best thing to claiming your soul for the Devil? Dragging your soul down so that you sin and live a worldly life focused on the desires of this earth rather than God and the things He has for us in eternity.

Matthew 6:19-20 (NKJV) reads, "Do not lay up for yourselves treasures on earth, where moth and rust destroy and where thieves break in and steal; but lay up for yourselves treasures in Heaven."

Satan's entire goal has been to drag others down with him. He would like nothing better than for you to stop thinking of God and letting the Holy Spirit rule your life. The more time you spend focusing on your possessions, the less time you spend reading the Bible. With so many temptations existing in the world today, what is a Christian to do? How can we hope to resist the temptations of Satan? After all, we're not Jesus, so we can't be expected to resist Satan, can we?

Carnal Christians often ignore their spiritual consciences. Satan has beaten them down so much that they just give up and give in to temptation. When you ignore the Holy Spirit that abides in you, you fall prey to worldly desires.

How often have you said, "Something told me not to do it," but you did it anyway? You violated your conscience and ignored the Holy Spirit's warning. We need to keep the Holy Spirit in mind. We need God. He does not need us to do anything for Him.

He loves us all, but if you refuse to surrender your life to Him, He will not give you salvation. If you do not repent and submit your life to Christ, you will continue to live outside His covenant—in bondage and wondering why you're miserable.

This is a carnal Christian's thought right now: *I'm good.* But you know the truth, and so does God. We are called to resist temptation.

James 4:1 and 7 (NKJV) reads, "Where do wars and fights come from among you? Do they not come from your desires for pleasure that war in you? Submit to God. Resist the devil, and he will flee from you."

That passage holds the answer to all of our temptation problems. There's nothing Satan fears more than a committed Christian who doesn't give in to temptation. Whenever you feel like the temptations are getting to be too much, the answer is never to give in. It may seem difficult in the short term, because giving in makes it seem like Satan is letting up on us, but in the long term our souls will suffer.

For a clue on how we can resist temptation, it's important to study what Jesus did when Satan tempted Him. The temptation of Jesus actually lasted for forty days. Take a few moments and answer these questions. They may just make you think about your future.

Be honest. Are you on your way to heaven?

- Are you too busy to carry someone else's burden?

- Are you frustrated with your life?

- Do you think your spouse causes all of your problems?

- Are you too busy to praise God?

- Do you have trouble forgiving others?

- Do you forgive but then refuse to forget?

- Do you listen to music or watch television more often than you listen to God?

- Do you dislike people you don't even know?

- Are you easily offended?

- Do you twist the words of others and create a story to justify your thoughts?

- Do you blame others when things go wrong?

- Do you dislike people because of their race?

- Are you in a same-sex relationship?

- Do you disrespect your children or spouse?

- Do you think you are going to heaven just because your parents or spouse are saved?

- Do you know the truth about Jesus but don't share it with others?

- Do you refuse to believe what God's Scriptures say in the Bible?

- Do you know the truth about Jesus but don't share it with others?

- Do you have to have everything your way?

- Are you being led by ungodly friends or spirits that influence you to do ungodly things?

- Do you lie to others to impress them?

- Do you think you have always been a child of God?

- If you died today, would you go to heaven?

This is what the Bible says in Luke 4:5 (NKJV):

> Then the devil took him up and revealed to him all the kingdoms of the world in a moment of time. He said, "I will give you the glory these kingdoms and authority over them." Then Satan said, "Because they are mine to give to anyone I please. I will give it all to you if you will worship me."

Now let's stop and think. Satan said "kingdoms of the world." That makes me think about people I know who are living carnally in this world and seem to be doing so well, but they are not following God's will. After reading this, it makes sense: those individuals only have a kingdom here on earth. So please do not be deceived by Satan's evil, worldly, materialistic scams.

Jesus replied, "The Scripture says, 'You must worship the Lord your God and serve only him.'" But Satan came back and offered Jesus the whole world if He would just worship him. Satan quoted Scripture to Jesus, twisting it to his evil purposes, just like he does today. Remember the fallen angels God threw out of heaven? Are they here on earth? Are they ruling your life? If God isn't, who is?

This might be a good time to analyze your spiritual condition and ask yourself which angel is leading you. Christians fall victim to all of forms of temptation, including the last one. The almighty God is the only one who can change your life and give grace—the key to eternity. If you don't understand anything else, get that part right for your salvation. Watch over your family and let no man or woman deceive you.

Luke 17:26-27 (NLT) says:

> When the Son of Man returns, it will be like it was in Noah's day. In those days before the flood, the people were enjoying banquets and parties and weddings right up to the time Noah entered his boat and the flood came to destroy them all.

People didn't realize what was going to happen until the flood came and swept them all away. That is the way it will be when Jesus returns. So you too must keep watch!

We often take time to seek worldly relationships. Why not build a relationship with God? It's time to focus on heaven, which is our future. Learning the Scriptures helps, especially when dealing with the fools in this world. There are devils walking around here on earth. It would be nice if they carried a pitchfork so we could see who they are, but they don't so we can't. Some are very beautiful and intelligent; they appear nice, but they are wolves in sheep's clothing.

Watch who you call your sister or brother until you know for sure you have the same Father

In Matthew 12:48-50 (NKJV), Jesus asked:

> Who are my brothers? Then he pointed to his disciples and said, "Look, these are my mother and brothers. Anyone who does the will of my Father in heaven is my brother and sister and mother!"

8

THE MANIFESTATION OF THE HOLY SPIRIT

For I am not ashamed of the gospel, because it is God's power for salvation to everyone who believes, first to the Jew, and also to the Greek. For in it God's righteousness is revealed from faith to faith, just as it is written: The righteous will live by faith.—Romans 1:16-17 (NKJV)

*T*HE HOLY SPIRIT DOESN'T ALWAYS MANIFEST Himself in dramatic ways like He did at Pentecost, but everyone should be able to see evidence of the Holy Spirit in each of us all of the time. After your conversion, both believers and nonbelievers should be able tell something different about you. Not different in a haughty, rude way but quiet obedience to God. It's a lifestyle change which begins with the indwelling power of the Holy Spirit

> Jesus says " I am the true vine, and My Father is the vinedresser. Every branch in Me that does not bear fruit He takes away; and every *branch* that bears fruit He prunes, that it may bear more fruit. You are already clean because of the word which I have spoken to you. Abide in Me, and I in you. As the branch cannot bear fruit of itself, unless it abides in the vine, neither can you, unless you abide in Me. Are you abiding in the things of this world, or the creator who created it? God said "I am the vine, you *are* the branches. He who abides in Me, and I in him, bears much fruit; for without Me you can do nothing. If anyone does not abide in Me, he is cast out as a branch and is withered; and they gather them and throw *them* into the fire, and they are burned. If you abide in Me, and My words abide in you, you will ask what you desire, and it shall be done for you. By this My Father is glorified, that you bear much fruit; **so you will be My disciples**. "As the Father loved Me, I also have loved you; abide in My love. If you keep My commandments, you will abide in My love, just as I have kept My Father's commandments and abide in His love. "These things I have spoken

to you, that My joy may remain in you, and *that* your joy may be full. This is My commandment, that you love one another as I have loved you. Greater love has no one than this, than to lay down one's life for his friends. You are My friends if you do whatever I command you. John 15:1-15 (NKJV)

God says we are to love one another! He says to love one another; as I have loved you. By this all will know that you are my disciples, if you have love for one another."

Now ask yourself this question... "Do I love my neighbor as myself?

Jesus washed the disciple's feet. **The bible tell us in John 13:7-17 (NKJV)**

Jesus said to Peter, "What I am doing you do not understand now, but you will know after this."

Peter said to Him, "You shall never wash my feet!" Jesus answered him, ***"If I do not wash you, you have no part with Me."***

Simon Peter said to Him, "Lord, not my feet only, but also my hands and my head!"

Jesus said to him, **"He who is bathed needs only to wash *his* feet,** but is completely clean; and you are clean, **but not all of you."** For He knew who would betray Him; therefore He said, **"You are not all clean."** So when He had washed their feet, taken His garments, and sat down again, He said to them, "Do you know what I have done to you? You call Me Teacher and Lord, and you say well, for so I am. If I then, your Lord and Teacher, have washed your feet, you also ought to wash one another's feet. For I have given you an example, that you should do as I have done to you. Most assuredly, I say to you, a servant is not greater than his master; nor is he who is sent greater than he who sent him. **If you know these things, blessed are you if you do them.**

The Christians who struggle with various lifestyles—including Homosexuality—are simply denying the Holy Spirit's work in their lives. Their Pride refuses to allow the Holy Spirit to direct their paths. Instead, they are governed by their emotions and desires allowing impure habits to manifest instead of the Holy Spirit.

The Bible tells us this in 1 Corinthians 6:12-20 (NLT)

"I am allowed to do anything"—but not everything is good for you. And even though "I am allowed to do anything," **I must not become a slave to anything**. You say, "Food was made for the stomach, and the stomach for food." (This is true, though someday God will do away with both of them.) But you can't say that our bodies were made for sexual immorality. They were made for the Lord, and the Lord cares about our bodies. And God will raise us from the dead by his power, just as he raised our Lord from the dead.

Don't you realize that your bodies are actually parts of Christ? Should a man take his body, which is part of Christ, and join it to a prostitute? Never! And don't you realize that if a man joins himself to a prostitute, he becomes one body with her? For the Scriptures say, "The two are united into one." But the person who is joined to the Lord is one spirit with him.

Run from sexual sin! No other sin so clearly affects the body as this one does. For sexual immorality is a sin against your own body. Don't you realize that your body is the temple of the Holy Spirit, who lives in you and was given to you by God? You do not belong to yourself, for God bought you with a high price. So you must honor God with your body.

Romans 1:21 (NKJV) reads, "For though they knew God, they did not glorify Him as God or show gratitude. Instead, their thinking became nonsense, and their senseless minds were darkened."

God has made the truth obvious to all of us through His creation, but some people choose to deny that truth and live however they want to live. God abandons these people to their sin, and the result is nonsense. These people trade the truth for a lie and decide to worship the things God created—instead of the worshipping the Creator Himself.

From the very beginning, God set forth a natural order of things, and the Holy Spirit manifests Himself by helping us keep this natural order. I recommend individuals who struggle with same-sex relationships to read Leviticus 18 and Romans 1:18-32 (NKJV).

Dr. Jack Graham is senior Pastor of Power Point Ministries. His 10 CD message series entitled~ Straight up will better prepare you to offer a bold biblical and compassionate response to some of the most important issues in our culture. Pastor Graham reminds us... as Christians, we are called to hate the sin and love the sinner, but loving the sinner does not mean we sit idly by while he or she lives a lifestyle that does not fit with the way the Bible says we should live.

1 Corinthians 6:9-11 (NKJV) reads:

> Do you not know that the unjust will not inherit God's kingdom? Do not be deceived: no sexually immoral people, idolaters, adulterers, male prostitutes, homosexuals, thieves, greedy people, drunkards, revilers, or swindlers will inherit God's kingdom.

Paul then goes on to say that some Christians lived these sorts of lives previously, but God sanctified them and changed them.

Our emotions are certainly a blessing from God, but Satan also uses them against us. Christians who struggle with same-sex relationships are victims of their own emotions, which Satan has used to indicate that they should have lustful thoughts for a member of the same sex. Homosexuality is only one example of this, however. Any of us can fall victim to our emotions at any time if we are not abiding in the Word.

Satan loves to put fear and doubt in our minds. He ruins relationships and can have us thinking all kinds of crazy thoughts. Guilt is one of Satan's terrible weapons that he uses to destroy our joy, our peace and our relationship with God. That's how Satan works. He will isolate you and guide you into sin. He is notorious for breaking up families and running scams. He loves to ruin relationships and confuse our minds about things—especially sex.

Believers should not get involved with either sins of the flesh or sins of the spirit, but those who are not guilty of "fleshly sins" (such as adultery, gluttony, etc.) should not condemn others; for they themselves may be guilty of sins of the spirit. The prodigal son in Luke 15 was guilty of sins of the flesh, but his proud, critical, unbending older brother was guilty of sins of the spirit.

What are sins of the spirit? Sins of the spirit: pride, stubbornness, gossip, jealousy, competition, bragging about results, etc. Pride is one of Satan's chief weapons. If Satan can get you to act and think independently of God's will, he can then control your will and control your life. You will think that you are acting freely, which is part of Satan's deception; but actually you will be acting under orders from the ruler of this world.

There's a bumper sticker you might have seen rolling around on cars near you. It reads, "Christians aren't perfect, just forgiven." The Bible tells us it's a fact that we all sin, but Christians know there is hope because they can ask for forgiveness.

Feeling jealous of others and living in a way God does not want you to live are heavy burdens to carry, as all sins are. God wants to take these burdens away. He's not going to do that, however, unless you ask for forgiveness. It's far too easy to live the lifestyle we want, just assuming that God will forgive us, but then never actually asking Him to. The only remedy is *forgiveness*. If someone wrongs you, forgive them. Jesus cautions us to be reconciled as quickly as possible. The longer you harbor an unforgiving spirit, the more territory Satan will gain in your life. Even if the other party does not forgive you. You may not be able to win them back into your life, but you can see to it that Satan is defeated in your own life. Jesus said teachers of religious laws like the Pharisees were like whitewashed tombs: beautiful on the outside but filled on the inside with the bones of the dead and other impurities. Outwardly, some of them looked like righteous people, but inwardly their hearts were filled with hypocrisy and lawlessness. Everything they did was for show.

The bible tells us Jesus references false prophets and signs during the Tribulation. The disciples asked Jesus when these things will happen. And what will be the sign of Your coming, and of the end of the age?

In Matthew 24:4-8 (NKJV):

> Jesus answered and said to them: "Take heed that no one deceives you. For many will come in My name, saying, 'I am the Christ,' and will deceive many. And you will hear of wars and rumors of wars. See that you are not troubled; for all these things must come to pass, but the end is not yet. For nation will rise against nation, and kingdom against kingdom. And there will be famines, pestilences, and earthquakes in various places. All these are the beginning of sorrows.

In 24:10-13 (NKJV):

> Many will be offended and shall betray one
> another and shall hate one another. Many false
> prophets shall rise and shall deceive many. Sin
> will be rampant, iniquity shall abound, and the
> love of many shall wax cold. But the one who
> endures the end shall be saved.

That sounds like the time we live in, doesn't it? But it is during moments of desperation, like what we experience every day, that we really begin to see what God is truly like. God wants us to ask Him for help, but the longer we wait, the harder our burdens become. It may seem difficult to ask God for help, but it's not impossible. The day you stop asking God for help is the day you start asking for trouble.

Ephesians 6:10-12 (NKJV) tells us to be strong in the Lord and in the power of His might. Put on the whole armor of God, that you may be able to stand against the wiles of the devil. For we do not wrestle against flesh and blood, but against principalities, against powers, against the rulers of the darkness of this age, against spiritual *hosts* of wickedness in the heavenly *places*. Every believer of Jesus Christ is indwelt by the Holy Spirit.

The fruit of the Spirit is not a list of behaviors you have to practice. Rather, it's a pattern for wholeness in life that you willingly adopt as you willingly submit to Christ in your life.

It is a fact, Christians will sin. Born again believers practice Sin-less. Sin leaves us broken hearted because we know that we grieved the Holy Spirit. *Dr. Arthur Belanger from the Open Bible Institutes* says a pattern of sin in the life of a believer hinders their fellowship with God and diminishes their confidence in the Word of God. Very often, Christians who have failed God want to enjoy fellowship with God again but are not sure how this can be realized. More often than not the parasite of guilt has done its damage and has left the Christian feeling absolutely hopeless.

Realizing Jesus Christ as our advocate is essential for the prospect of restoration and recovery (1 John 2:1 NKJV) The terminology of advocate represents the idea of a lawyer who represents his client before a court of law. From a biblical perspective, it presents Christ Jesus as the single defense for the believer who sins and brings the repentant believer back to fellowship with God the Father. The sole basis of Christ advocacy is the work He accomplished on the cross... namely, His shed blood and death. **A Christian can never be restored to fellowship with God by virtue of a promise or willingness to do better.** The only basis why God is justified to forgive the Christian is the death of His Son Jesus Christ. Our relationship to God is made sure by His grace (Ephesians 2:8-9 NKJV) and our fellowship can only be made secured by grace. God's grace compels the sinning believer to rely upon Jesus as the advocate for the remission of their sin. **Christ Jesus can only advocate for us effectively by virtue of His shed blood.** When a Christian repents from their sin and confesses their sin and sorrow to Christ, fellowship is restored instantly (1 John 1:9 NKJV). Forgiveness is instant.... cleansing is

constant. God not only restores the Christian to fellowship with
Him... He begins the process of recovery from the consequence of
sin. **The advocacy of Christ not only restores us~He enables us to
recover.** This is why a Christian will never be hopeless.

9

THE HOLY SPIRIT

While Peter was still speaking these words,
the Holy Spirit fell upon all those who heard
the word. And those of the circumcision who
believed were astonished, as many as came with
Peter, because the gift of the Holy Spirit had
been poured out on the Gentiles also. For they
heard them speak with tongues and magnify
God.

—Acts 10:44-46 NKJV

*T*HE BIBLE URGES US TO BE HOLY. JESUS
commands us to be holy because He is holy, but there
seems to be a basic misunderstanding about what
this means for a number of Christians today. As Christians,
we know that God has promised the Holy Spirit to us, but we

have no idea when we will receive Him. In the first chapter of the book of Acts, Jesus promises the Holy Spirit to believers in Jerusalem, but He also says that they will have to wait a very short time.

Acts 1:1-8 (NIV):

> In my former book, Theophilus, I wrote about all that Jesus began to do and to teach until the day he was taken up to heaven, after giving instructions through the Holy Spirit to the apostles he had chosen. After his suffering, he presented himself to them and gave many convincing proofs that he was alive. He appeared to them over a period of forty days and spoke about the kingdom of God. On one occasion, while he was eating with them, he gave them this command: 'Do not leave Jerusalem, but wait for the gift my Father promised, which you have heard me speak about. For John baptized with water, but in a few days you will be baptized with the Holy Spirit.'

> Then they gathered round him and asked him, 'Lord, are you at this time going to restore the kingdom to Israel?'

He said to them: 'It is not for you to know the times or dates the Father has set by his own authority. But you will receive power when the Holy Spirit comes on you; and you will be my witnesses in Jerusalem, and in all Judea and Samaria, and to the ends of the earth.'

So God has promised us the Holy Spirit, but, as with everything else in life, it is not for us to know the day or the hour when we will receive it. We can't know when God will restore us, but we do have His promise that He will.

I recall the day I was baptized. I really looked up to the women in that church. They always dressed modestly and didn't wear any jewelry. The moment I stepped up and out of that baptismal font, one of them said to me, "Now don't you want to take those gold earrings off?"

In that precise moment, I was dripping wet from the waters of baptism, but I was still a baby Christian still carnal. Not to mention their was a lot of legalism in the church at that time. We could not wear make-up, jewelry, or slacks. Legalism is the elevation of man-made tradition to be equal to the commands of God. It is the belief that keeping these traditions will earn you favor with God. Legalism is a religious spirit that leads people to believe that not worshiping a certain way or following a particular liturgy or performing precise rituals means you are not a good Christian. Naturally, you want to follow the Word of

God and you don't want to get so undisciplined that you cross over into carnality.

Christians should refrain from sin and observe the law; however, some Christians become so focused on the law they forget the overarching role of grace and love. Jesus paid the ultimate price, dying on a cross so He could free us from the law through His mercy and grace. The human spirit is a facet of human personality; the Holy Spirit who comes to indwell the believer at conversion is a Person. Notice James 2:26 (NKJV) ~

> As the body without the spirit is dead, so faith without deeds is dead. Paul also says in 1 Corinthians 2:11-15 (NKJV) For what man knows the things of a man except the spirit of the man which is in him? Even so no one knows the things of God except the Spirit of God. Now we have received, not the spirit of the world, but the Spirit who is from God, that we might know the things that have been freely given to us by God. These things we also speak, not in words which man's wisdom teaches but which the Holy Spirit teaches, comparing spiritual things with spiritual. But the natural man does not receive the things of the Spirit of God, for they are foolishness to him; nor can he know *them*, because they are spiritually discerned.

I had asked Jesus to be my Savior, but I had not yet received the Holy Spirit. I've noticed people don't really mention praying in the Spirit very often.

There is a difference between baby Christians and Christians who have received the Holy Spirit. Baby Christians are still learning and have not yet matured to the place where they understand about being filled with the Spirit. They may still live worldly lives because they have not been filled with the Holy Spirit, but Christians who reject the worldly life and yearn to be filled with Spirit will be blessed with His fire.

Acts 2 has the story of the very first coming of the Holy Spirit. Most Christians know the story from all of the drama that comes with it: tongues of fire on their heads, speaking in tongues, and a rushing wind. But have you actually read the story recently? Take a moment and read all of Acts 2. You'll see not only the dramatic coming of the Holy Spirit at Pentecost but also evidence of lives that were changed drastically. The gospel spread like wildfire. When the Holy Spirit came and rested on the mature Christians, they suddenly began to testify and tell others about Christ. Three thousand baby Christians were born. The mature Christians also began to work miracles in God's name. These Christians were on fire for God, and that fire continued to burn as they spread the gospel.

Even today we see evidence of what God does when people are on fire for Him. Christians are actually persecuted in some countries as the governments try to wipe out their faith. But faith in Christ can't be wiped out. Christians who have been filled with the Holy Spirit are able to spread the gospel even when they are looking death right in the face. Only Christians who are on fire with the Holy Spirit have the strength to stand up to such adversity. Stop and think for a moment what you would say if someone asked if you believed in God. Now what if they threatened to cut off both of your hands with an axe if you professed God? This is pretty heavy stuff.

Even in the book of Acts, we see threats for people to stop speaking the name of God and preaching about Him. But what did Peter and John do? The Jewish leaders at the time were worried because Peter and John had been performing miracles in Jesus's name after receiving the Holy Spirit. They ordered Peter and John not to "preach or teach at all in the name of Jesus."

Acts 4:19 (NKJV) :

> But Peter and John answered them, "Whether it's right in the sight of God for us to listen to you rather than to God, you decide; for we are unable to stop speaking about what we have seen and heard."

Christians who have the Holy Spirit living in them are unable to stop spreading the gospel, both in word and in deed. It doesn't mean that they don't make mistakes from time to time, but they are guided by the Holy Spirit to walk in obedience according to His commandments. If they do sin it weighs heavily on their hearts.

Will born again believers continue in Sin?

The apostle John taught in his first epistle that born again believers will not continue in sin (1 John 5:18-20) NKJV. Therefore, is it possible for a born again Christian to live in a continued pattern of sin which reflects a disposition to behave in a manner that grieves the Holy Spirit internally and corrupts one's testimony externally? The short answer is no. Why? First, there is no pattern or precedence in the Bible that would even suggest the possibility. It is true, however, the scriptures record Christians sinning against God. With each recording God chastens His rebellious children by using consequential principles to the point of their repentance. King David is a classic example and the parable of the prodigal son also demonstrates God's work in the life of His redeemed children in a parental context.

Secondly, Born again Christians are dead to sin Roman 6:1-2 (NKJV). Paul taught that we as believers are dead to the sin nature or the Adamic nature. Literally, again Christians are free from the enslaving power of the sin nature and we are by God's power, enabled to overcome the propensity of our sinful nature by God's grace through faith 1 John 5:4-5 (NKJV) The relationship one is privileged to have with Jesus Christ is deeper than any relationship the human mind has ever or could ever realize. Salvation by

God's grace gifts the Christian with the mind of Christ and the indwelling of the Holy Spirit which is both personal and perpetual. One of the most important aspects of God's grace is the gift of inseparability (Romans 8:38-39)(Romans 6:1-2) NKJV. As a believer, you can be sure that the Holy Spirit will be assertive within your spirit when confronted with a situation or decision that would take you outside the will of God.

As John 14:26 NKJV tells us, "But the Counselor, the Holy Spirit—the Father will send Him in My Name—will teach you all things and remind you of everything I have told you." Instead of seeing the world through rose-colored glasses, Christians see it through God-colored glasses. It's imperative that we know and believe the truth about Jesus Christ and the life he lived on this earth. John 14:6 (NIV) Jesus said, "I am the way the truth and the life. No one comes to the Father except through me.

10

ABIDING DAILY
IN CHRIST

For by grace you have been saved through faith, and
that not of yourselves; it is the gift of God, not of
works, lest anyone should boast.

—Ephesians 2:8 (NKJV)

*B*EING LOST CAN BE A TERRIFYING EXPE-
rience. I remember once when I was about six or
seven years old, my sister and I got lost on our way
home from school. We had just moved to the neighborhood,
so we didn't know our way around. It also wasn't the best
neighborhood at the time. We were living in the inner city of
Indianapolis, Indiana. (It was temporary housing, and we moved
to a better home a short while later.) The night we got lost, my
sister and I wandered around the city streets. She actually picked

me up and put me on her shoulders because I was crying. After several hours, we finally saw my father and four brothers. They were out looking for us—God led them straight to us. In those days, I was truly lost in so many ways; I didn't know God yet, but He was still taking care of me. He was abiding in my life even though I had not yet made the choice to trust Him.

God thinks of each one of us every moment of the day. He is timeless, and His love is also timeless. What an amazing gift! Just as God abides in us all of the time, He wants us to learn to abide in Him all of the time. It's like living in a constant awareness of God and all of His glory.

Throughout history, there have been many stories of people who lived in a constant awareness of God—some in the Bible and others after biblical times. For someone like Moses, God's presence was quite literal. In fact, he had to wear a veil over his face after he came down from Mount Sinai after spending time with God, because God's glory was so great that it made his face shine brightly and people couldn't look at it.

So how can we begin to abide in Christ every moment of every day? It starts the moment your eyes pop open in the morning. Strive to give your first thought of the day to God. Think about what He has planned for you each day rather than what your plans are. Praying the Model Prayer (Matthew 6:9-13) NKJV,

Pastor Suzette T. Caldwell reminds us that God's people are required to pray efficacious, powerful prayers. She states in her book—Praying to Change Your Life that so many Christians have a lackluster, ineffective prayer life because they do not incorporate the Scriptures into their prayers. When you use the Word of God in your prayers, you will experience positive results. Suzette T. Caldwell has studied and taught prayer for 18 years. She is the Associate Pastor for Windsor Village United Methodist Church and Board Chairman for the Kingdom Builders Prayer Institute. Her book is a must have if you are serious about revolutionizing and increasing the power of your prayer life.

This step may be a bit more difficult for some than it is for others, especially if you are one of those people who is extremely groggy when you first wake up, but you will adjust with time. Pray the Lord's Prayer and ask God to give you the strength to feel His presence at every moment.

Going to church is important for fellowship, but Christians who don't study the Word of God for themselves can only maintain a very distant relationship with Him. Think of it as the difference between actually spending time with someone and reading a letter from her once in a while. When you actually invite your friend into your home, you get the chance to talk with her and hear how she's doing, directly from her own lips. But if you rely only on receiving a letter from her once in a while, then you run the risk of that letter becoming damaged or destroyed in the mail. You can only truly have a relationship if you actually spend time together. The more time you spend together, the closer you will become.

In the same way, you risk God's message becoming damaged before it gets to you if you don't take the time to read it for yourself. Human beings make mistakes, and God has warned us about false prophets. If you yourself read what the Bible says, you will discover God's presence in a way you never could have imagined.

The more you read it, the more easily you will be able to recall Scriptures at any given time. Not only will God's Word literally be living inside you, but you will be overflowing with it. Just like Paul and the early Christians, you won't be able to stop telling others about God and showing them how He has changed your life. You will become a contagious Christian rather than a carnal Christian.

Think about how different the world would be if everyone had the characteristics of Christ, traits which the Holy Spirit desires to put in us. The Bible tells us this in 1 Corinthians 3 (NKJV):

> And I, brethren, could not speak to you as to spiritual *people* but as to carnal, as to babes in Christ. I fed you with milk and not with solid food; for until now you were not able *to receive it*, and even now you are still not able; for you are still carnal. For where *there are* envy, strife, and divisions among you, are you not carnal and behaving like

mere men? For when one says, "I *am* of Paul," and another, "I am of Apollos," are you not carnal?

Who then is Paul, and who is Apollos, but ministers through whom you believed, as the Lord gave to each one? I planted, Apollos watered, but God gave the increase. So then neither he who plants is anything, nor he who waters, but God who gives the increase. Now he who plants and he who waters are one, and each one will receive his own reward according to his own labor.

For we are God's fellow workers; you are God's field, *you are* God's building. According to the grace of God which was given to me, as a wise master builder I have laid the foundation, and another builds on it. But let each one take heed how he builds on it. For no other foundation can anyone lay than that which is laid, which is Jesus Christ. Now if anyone builds on this foundation *with* gold, silver, precious stones, wood, hay, straw, each one's work will become clear; for the Day will declare it, because it will be revealed by fire; and the fire will test each one's work, of what sort it is. If anyone's work which he has built on *it* endures, he will receive a reward. If anyone's work is burned, he will suffer loss; but he himself will be saved, yet so as through fire.

Do you not know that you are the temple of God and *that* the Spirit of God dwells in you? If anyone defiles the temple of God, God will destroy him. For the *temple* of God is holy, which temple you are.

Let no one deceive himself. If anyone among you seems to be wise in this age, let him become a fool that he may become wise. For the wisdom of this world is foolishness with God. For it is written, "He catches the wise in their *own* craftiness"; and again, "The LORD knows the thoughts of the wise, that they are futile." Therefore let no one boast in men. For all things are yours: whether Paul or Apollos or Cephas, or the world or life or death, or things present or things to come—all are yours. And you *are* Christ's, and Christ *is* God's.

As I close, I want to share these godly truths from Paul, an apostle of Jesus Christ from the book of Ephesians:

Ephesians 4:29-32 (NLT)

Don't use foul or abusive language. Let everything you say be good and helpful, so that your words will be an encouragement to those who hear them.

And do not bring sorrow to God's Holy Spirit by the way you live. Remember, he has identified you as his own, guaranteeing that you will be saved on the day of redemption.

Get rid of all bitterness, rage, anger, harsh words, and slander, as well as all types of evil behavior. Instead, be kind to each other, tenderhearted, forgiving one another, just as God through Christ has forgiven you.

I ask that you keep these few final Bible verses in your heart.

Isaiah 1:19-20 (NKJV)

If you are willing and obedient, You shall eat the good of the land; But if you refuse and rebel,

You shall be devoured by the sword"; For the mouth of the Lord has spoken.

Seal it in your memory and carry it with you always.

John 14:6 (NKJV)

Jesus said~ "I am the way, the truth, and the life. No one comes to the Father except through Me."

25 REASONS TO ABIDE IN GOD'S WORD

1. Abiding in God's Word leads to commitment and obedience.

Deuteronomy 6:4-8 (NLT)

> The Lord is our God, and you must love the Lord your God with all your heart, all your soul, and all your strength. We must commit ourselves wholeheartedly to these commands. Repeat them again and again to your children. Talk about them when you are at home and when you are on the road, when you are going to bed and when you are getting up. Tie them to your hands and wear them on your forehead as reminders.

2. Abiding in God's Word tells us to put on the whole armor of God.

Ephesians 6:10-13 (NKJV)

> Be strong in the Lord and in the power of His might. Put on the whole armor of God, that you may be able to stand against the wiles of the devil. For we do not wrestle against flesh and blood, but against principalities, against powers, against the rulers of the darkness of this age, against spiritual hosts of wickedness in the heavenly places. Therefore take up the whole armor of God, that you may be able to withstand in the evil day, and having done all, to stand.

3. Abiding in God's Word unites us joyfully.

Philippians 4:6-7 (NKJV)

> Be anxious for nothing, but in everything by prayer and supplication, with thanksgiving, let your requests be made known to God; and the peace of God, which surpasses all understanding, will guard your hearts and minds through Christ Jesus.

4. Abiding in God's Word encourages us to meditate on godly things.

Philippians 4:8 (NKJV)

> Whatever things are true, whatever things are noble, whatever things are just, whatever things are pure, whatever things are lovely, whatever things are of good report, if there is any virtue and if there is anything praiseworthy—meditate on these things.

5. Abiding in God's Word will reveals perilous times.

2 Timothy 3:1-7 (NKJV)

> Know this, that in the last days perilous times will come. For men will be lovers of themselves, lovers of money, boasters, proud, blasphemers, disobedient to parents, unthankful, unholy, unloving, unforgiving, slanderers, without self-control, brutal, despisers of good, traitors, headstrong, haughty, lovers of pleasure rather than lovers of God, having a form of godliness but denying its power. And from such people turn away! For of this sort are those who creep into households and make captives of gullible

women loaded down with sins, led away by various lusts, always learning and never able to come to the knowledge of the truth.

6. Abiding in God's Word gives us grace for His glory.

Romans 6:15-18 (NLT)

> Well then, since God's grace has set us free from the law, does that mean we can go on sinning? Of course not! Don't you realize that you become the slave of whatever you choose to obey? You can be a slave to sin, which leads to death, or you can choose to obey God, which leads to righteous living. Thank God! Once you were slaves of sin, but now you wholeheartedly obey this teaching we have given you. Now you are free from your slavery to sin, and you have become slaves to righteous living.

7. Abiding in God's Word keeps us alert.

1 Peter 5:8-11 (NKJV)

> Be sober, be vigilant; because your adversary the devil walks about like a roaring lion, seeking whom he may devour. Resist him, steadfast in the faith, knowing that the same sufferings are

experienced by your brotherhood in the world. But may the God of all grace, who called us to His eternal glory by Christ Jesus, after you have suffered a while, perfect, establish, strengthen, and settle you.

8.   Abiding in God's Word reveals truth.

1 John 3:7-14 (NKJV)

Little children, let no one deceive you. He who practices righteousness is righteous, just as He is righteous. He who sins is of the devil, for the devil has sinned from the beginning. For this purpose the Son of God was manifested, that He might destroy the works of the devil. Whoever has been born of God does not sin, for His seed remains in him; and he cannot sin, because he has been born of God. In this the children of God and the children of the devil are manifest: Whoever does not practice righteousness is not of God, nor is he who does not love his brother. For this is the message that you heard from the beginning, that we should love one another, not as Cain who was of the wicked one and murdered his brother. And why did he murder him? Because his works were evil and his brother's righteous. Do not marvel, my brethren, if the world hates you. We know that we have passed from death to life, because we love the brethren. He who does not love his brother abides in death.

9. Abiding in God's Word makes us wise. Proverbs 15:31-33 (NKJV)

> The ear that hears the rebukes of life Will abide among the wise. He who disdains instruction despises his own soul, but he who heeds rebuke gets understanding. The fear of the LORD is the instruction of wisdom. And before honor is humility.

10. Abiding in God's Word is the only way to heaven.

John 14:6 (NKJV)

> Jesus said to him, "I am the way, the truth, and the life. No one comes to the Father except through Me."

11. Abiding in God's Word reminds us to keep his commandments.

John 15:15-17 (NKJV)

> No longer do I call you servants, for a servant does not know what his master is doing; but I have called you friends, for all things that I heard from My Father I have made known to you. You did not choose Me, but I chose you and appointed you that you should go and bear fruit, and that your fruit should remain, that whatever you ask the Father in My name He may give you. These things I command you, that you love one another.

12. Abiding in God's Word is the indwelling truth of the Father and the Son.

John 14:23-24 (NKJV)

> Jesus answered and said to him, "If anyone loves Me, he will keep My word; and My Father will love him, and We will come to him and make Our home with him. He who does not love Me does not keep My words; and the word which you hear is not Mine but the Father's who sent Me."

13. Abiding in God's Word reminds us to stay sober.

Ephesians 5:18-20 (NKJV)

> And do not be drunk with wine, in which is dissipation; but be filled with the Spirit, speaking to one another in psalms and hymns and spiritual songs, singing and making melody in your heart to the Lord, giving thanks always for all things to God the Father in the name of our Lord Jesus Christ, submitting to one another in the fear of God.

14. Abiding in God's Word tells the truth about this world.

1 John 2:15-17 (NLT)

> Do not love this world nor the things it offers you, for when you love the world, you do not have the love of the Father in you. For the world offers only a craving for physical pleasure, a craving for everything we see, and pride in our achievements and possessions. These are not from the Father, but are from this world. And this world is fading away, along with everything that people crave. But anyone who does what pleases God will live forever.

15. Abiding in God's Word reveals the Antichrist.

1 John 2:22-23 (NKJV)

> Who is a liar but he who denies that Jesus is the
> Christ? He is antichrist who denies the Father
> and the Son. Whoever denies the Son does not
> have the Father either; he who acknowledges the
> Son has the Father also.

16. Abiding in God's Word informs us about communion.

1 Corinthians 11:27-30 (NLT)

> So anyone who eats this bread or drinks this
> cup of the Lord unworthily is guilty of sinning
> against the body and blood of the Lord. That is
> why you should examine yourself before eating
> the bread and drinking the cup. For if you eat
> the bread or drink the cup without honoring
> the body of Christ, you are eating and drinking
> God's judgment upon yourself. That is why
> many of you are weak and sick and some have
> even died.

17. Abiding in God's Word allows the Holy Spirit to guide.

Galatians 5:16-26 (NLT)

> Let the Holy Spirit guide your lives. Then you won't be doing what your sinful nature craves. The sinful nature wants to do evil, which is just the opposite of what the Spirit wants. And the Spirit gives us desires that are the opposite of what the sinful nature desires. These two forces are constantly fighting each other, so you are not free to carry out your good intentions. But when you are directed by the Spirit, you are not under obligation to the Law of Moses. When you follow the desires of your sinful nature, the results are very clear: sexual immorality, impurity, lustful pleasures, idolatry, sorcery, hostility, quarreling, jealousy, outbursts of anger, selfish ambition, dissension, division, envy, drunkenness, wild parties, and other sins like these. Let me tell you again, as I have before, that anyone living that sort of life will not inherit the kingdom of God. But the Holy Spirit produces this kind of fruit in our lives: love, joy, peace, patience, kindness, goodness, faithfulness, gentleness, and self-control. There is no law against these

things! Those who belong to Christ Jesus have nailed the passions and desires of their sinful nature to his cross and crucified them there. Since we are living by the Spirit, let us follow the Spirit's leading in every part of our lives. Let us not become conceited, or provoke one another, or be jealous of one another.

18. Abiding in God's Word teaches to avoid lawlessness.

1 John 3:4-9 (NKJV)

Whomever commits sin also commits lawlessness, and sin is lawlessness. And you know that He was manifested to take away our sins, and in Him there is no sin. Whoever abides in Him does not sin. Whoever sins has neither seen Him nor known Him. Little children, let no one deceive you. He who practices righteousness is righteous, just as He is righteous. He who sins is of the devil, for the devil has sinned from the beginning. For this purpose the Son of God was manifested, that He might destroy the works of the devil. Whoever has been born of God does not sin, for His seed remains in him; and he cannot sin, because he has been born of God.

19. Abiding in God's Word gives us discernment.

1 John 4:1-6 (NLT)

> Do not believe everyone who claims to speak by the Spirit. You must test them to see if the spirit they have comes from God. For there are many false prophets in the world. This is how we know if they have the Spirit of God: If a person claiming to be a prophet acknowledges that Jesus Christ came in a real body, that person has the Spirit of God. But if someone claims to be a prophet and does not acknowledge the truth about Jesus, that person is not from God. Such a person has the spirit of the Antichrist, which you heard is coming into the world and indeed is already here. But you belong to God, my dear children. You have already won a victory over those people, because the Spirit who lives in you is greater than the spirit who lives in the world. Those people belong to this world, so they speak from the world's viewpoint, and the world listens to them. But we belong to God, and those who know God listen to us. If they do not belong to God, they do not listen to us. That is how we know if someone has the Spirit of truth or the spirit of deception.

20. Abiding in God's Word tells us about love, prophecy, and tongues.

1 Corinthians 14:1-5 (NKJV)

> Pursue love, and desire spiritual gifts, but especially that you may prophesy. For he who speaks in a tongue does not speak to men but to God, for no one understands him; however, in the spirit he speaks mysteries. But he who prophesies speaks edification and exhortation and comfort to men. He who speaks in a tongue edifies himself, but he who prophesies edifies the church. I wish you all spoke with tongues, but even more that you prophesied; for he who prophesies is greater than he who speaks with tongues, unless indeed he interprets, that the church may receive edification

21. Abiding in God's Word reveals spiritual gifts.

Ephesians 4:5-7 (NLT)

> There is one Lord, one faith, one baptism, and one God and Father, who is over all and in all and living through all. However, he has given each one of us a special gift through the generosity of Christ.

1 Corinthians 12:7-11 (NLT)

> A spiritual gift is given to each of us so we can
> help each other. To one person the Spirit gives
> the ability to give wise advice, to another the
> same Spirit gives a message of special knowledge.
> The same Spirit gives great faith to another,
> and to someone else the one Spirit gives the
> gift of healing. He gives one person the power
> to perform miracles, and another the ability to
> prophesy. He gives someone else the ability to
> discern whether a message is from the Spirit
> of God or from another spirit. Still another
> person is given the ability to speak in unknown
> languages, while another is given the ability to
> interpret what is being said. It is the one and
> only Spirit who distributes all these gifts. He
> alone decides which gift each person should
> have.

22. Abiding in God's Word allows us how to see God through
    love.

1 John 4:12-21 (NKJV)

> There is no fear in love; but perfect love casts
> out fear, because fear involves torment. But he
> who fears has not been made perfect in love. We

love Him because He first loved us. If someone says, "I love God," and hates his brother, he is a liar; for he who does not love his brother whom he has seen, how can he love God whom he has not seen? And this commandment we have from Him: that he who loves God must love his brother.

23. Abiding in God's Words reminds us to live as childrenin the light.

Ephesians 4:17-19 (NLT)

> With the Lord's authority I say this: Live no longer as the Gentiles do, for they are hopelessly confused. Their minds are full of darkness; they wander far from the life God gives because they have closed their minds and hardened their hearts against him. They have no sense of shame. They live for lustful pleasure and eagerly practice every kind of impurity.

24. Abiding in God's Word encourages righteousness.

Ephesians 4:28-32 (NKJV)

> Let him who stole steal no longer, but rather let him labor, working with his hands what is

good, that he may have something to give him who has need. Let no corrupt word proceed out of your mouth, but what is good for necessary edification, that it may impart grace to the hearers. And do not grieve the Holy Spirit of God, by whom you were sealed for the day of redemption. Let all bitterness, wrath, anger, clamor, and evil speaking be put away from you, with all malice. And be kind to one another, tenderhearted, forgiving one another, even as God in Christ forgave you.

25. Abiding in God's Word tells us to fight the good fight of faith. 1 Timothy 6:11-14 (ESV)

But as for you, O man of God, flee these things. Pursue righteousness, godliness, faith, love, steadfastness, gentleness. Fight the good fight of the faith. Take hold of the eternal life to which you were called and about which you made the good confession in the presence of many witnesses. I charge you in the presence of God, who gives life to all things, and of Christ Jesus, who in his testimony before Pontius Pilate made the good confession, to keep the commandment unstained and free from reproach until the appearing of our Lord Jesus Christ.

THE TEN COMMANDMENTS

Exodus 20: 1-17 (NLT)

Then God gave the people all these instructions. "I am the LORD your God, who rescued you from the land of Egypt, the place of your slavery.

I.

You must not have any other God but me.

2.

You must not make for yourself an idol of any kind, or an image of anything in the heavens or on the earth or in the sea. You must not bow down to them or worship them, for I,

the Lord your God, am a jealous God who will not tolerate
your affection for any other gods. I lay the sins of the parents
upon their children; the entire family is affected—even
children in the third and fourth generations of those
who reject me. But I lavish unfailing love for a thousand
generations on those who love me and obey my commands.

3.

You must not misuse the name of the Lord your God. The
Lord will not let you go unpunished if you misuse his name.

4.

Remember to observe the Sabbath day by keeping it holy . . . ,
That is why the Lord blessed the Sabbath day and set it apart
as holy.

5.

Honor your father and mother. Then you will live a long, full
life in the land the Lord your God is giving you.

6.

You must not murder.

7.

You must not commit adultery.

8.

You must not steal.

9.

You must not testify falsely against your neighbor.

10.

You must not covet your neighbor's house. You must not covet
your neighbor's wife, male or female servant,
ox or donkey, or anything else that belongs to your neighbor.

Romans 8:1-11 (NKJV)

Free from Indwelling Sin

There is therefore now no condemnation to those who are in Christ Jesus, who do not walk according to the flesh, but according to the Spirit. For the law of the Spirit of life in Christ Jesus has made me free from the law of sin and death. For what the law could not do in that it was weak through the flesh, God did by sending His own Son in the likeness of sinful flesh, on account of sin: He condemned sin in the flesh, that the righteous requirement of the law might be fulfilled in us who do not walk according to the flesh but according to the Spirit. For those who live according to the flesh set their minds on the things of the flesh, but those who live according to the Spirit, the things of the Spirit. For to be carnally minded is death, but to be spiritually minded is life and peace. Because the carnal mind is enmity against God; for it is not subject to the law of God, nor indeed can be. So then, those who are in the flesh cannot please God. But you are not in the flesh but in the Spirit, if indeed the Spirit of God dwells in you. Now if anyone does not have the Spirit of Christ, he is not His. And if Christ is in you, the body is dead because of sin, but the Spirit is life because of righteousness. But if the Spirit of Him who raised Jesus from the dead dwells in you, He who raised Christ from the dead will also give life to your mortal bodies through His Spirit who dwells in you.

Abide in me, and I in you.
As the branch cannot
bear fruit by itself unless
it abides in the vine,
neither can you,
unless you abide in me.

—John 15:4 (NKJV)

Printed in the United States
By Bookmasters